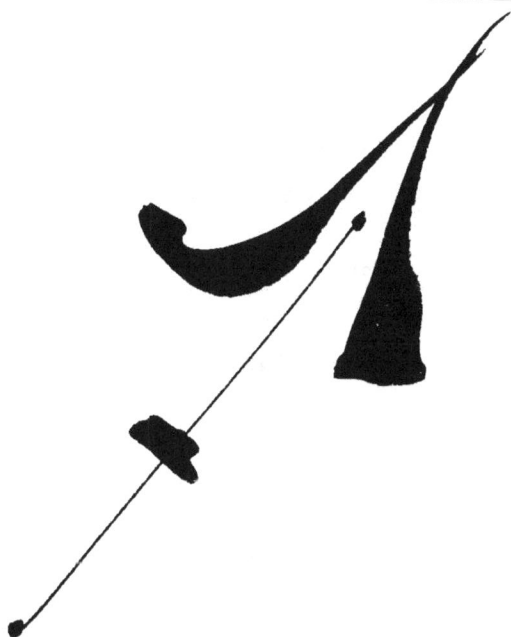

MUDRAS

for

SAGITTARIUS

By Sabrina Mesko Ph.D.H.

A Mudra Hands™ Book
Published by Mudra Hands Publishing

Copyright © 2013 Sabrina Mesko Ph.D.H.

Photography by Mara
Animal photography by Sabrina Mesko
Illustrations by Kiar Mesko
Cover photo by Mara

Printed in the United States of America

ISBN-13:978-0615920948
ISBN-10: 0615920942

For all my Sagittarius Friends

TABLE OF CONTENTS

Introduction   12
MUDRA   16
Instructions for Practice   16
Breath Control   17
Chakras   18
Nadis   21
Your Hands and Fingers   22
Mantra   22
About Astrology   23
Your Sun Sign   24
Your Rising Sign   25
How to use this book   25

MUDRAS for TRANSCENDING CHALLENGES   27
MUDRA of Good Speech   28
MUDRA for Patience   30
MUDRA for Preventing Exhaustion   32

MUDRAS for Your HEALTH AND BEAUTY   35
MUDRA for Strong Nerves   36
MUDRA for Recharging   38
MUDRA for Preventing Burnout   40

MUDRAS for LOVE   43
MUDRA for Opening Your Heart   44
MUDRA for Facing Fear   46
MUDRA for Guidance   48

MUDRAS for SUCCESS   51
MUDRA for Rejuvenation   52
MUDRA for Prosperity   54
MUDRA for Mental Balance   56

About the Author   59

THE MUDRA PRACTICE IS A
COMPLIMENTARY HEALING TECHNIQUE,
THAT OFFERS FAST AND EFFECTIVE
POSITIVE RESULTS.

MUDRAS WORK HARMONIOUSLY
WITH OTHER TRADITIONAL,
ALTERNATIVE AND COMPLEMENTARY
HEALING PROTOCOLS.

THEY HELP RESTORE DEPLETED
SUBTLE ENERGY STATES
AND OPTIMIZE THE PRACTITIONER'S
OVERALL STATE OF WELLNESS.

Mudras for

SAGITTARIUS

NOVEMBER 23 - DECEMBER 21

BODY
Hips, thighs, liver

PLANET
Jupiter

COLORS
Dark blue, purple

ELEMENT
Fire

STONES and GEMS
Topaz

ANIMAL
Horse, deer

INTRODUCTION

Ever since I can remember, I have been fascinated by the never ending view of the stars in the sky and the presence of other mysterious planets. As a child I wondered for hours about where does the Universe end and when my Father explained the possibility that time and space exist in a very different way than we imagined, my mind went wild with possibilities. I was however quite skeptical about astrology in general until one day in my early youth, a dear friend introduced me to a true Master of Vedic Astrology. He quickly and completely diminished any of my doubts about how precise certain facts can be revealed in one's Celestial map.

It was as if an invisible veil had been removed, and I was granted a peek over to the other side. The astrologer also adamantly pointed out that nothing is written in stone and one's destiny has a lot of space to navigate thru. You can make the best of the situation if you know your given parameters. My fascination and use of astrological science continues to this day and compliments and enriches my work with other observation techniques that I use when consulting.

One is born with character aspects and potential for realization of mapped-out future events, but there is always a possibility that another road may be taken. This has to do with the choices we make. Free will is given to all of us, even though often the choices we have seem to be very limited. But still, the choices are always there, forcing us to consciously participate and eventually take responsibility for our decisions, actions, and consequences.

The science of Astrology has been around for millenniums and even though some people are still doubtful, I always remind them that there is no disputing the fact, that the Moon affects the high and low tide of our Oceans - hence our bodies consisting mostly of water are affected by planetary movements in many fascinating and profound ways. Even the biggest skeptic agrees with that fact.

The Love of the Universal Power for each one of us is unconditional, everlasting and omnipresent. No matter what kind of life-journey you have, it is the very best one designed especially for you, rest assured. And when you are experiencing life's various challenges and wishing for a smooth ride instead, keep in mind that a life filled with lessons is a life fulfilling its purpose. The tests you encounter in your daily life are your opportunities.The wisdom learned is your asset, and the experiences gained are your wealth. Your Spirit's abundance is measured by the battles you fought and how you fought them. Did you help others and leave this world a better place in any way? Your true intention matters more than you know.

Each one of us has a very unique-one of a kind celestial map placed gently, but firmly and irrevocably into effect at the precise time of our birth. There are certain aspects of one's chart that reveal possible character tendencies and predisposed behavior in regards to love, partnerships, maintaining one's health, pursuit of success and a way of communicating. The benefits of knowing and understanding the effects of your chart on various aspects of your life can be profound. It can help you understand and prepare ahead of time for certain circumstances that are coming your way, which increases the possibility of a better quality of life in general.

If you knew that a specific time period could be beneficial for your career wouldn't it be good to know that ahead of your plans? If you are aware that certain aspects of your physical constitution are predisposed to a weakness or sensitivity, wouldn't it be beneficial to pay attention and prevent a possible future health ailment?

If you can foresee that a certain time will be slower for you in achieving positive results, wouldn't it be wise to use that time for preparation for a more fortuitous timing? How many times have you attempted to pursue a dream of yours that just didn't seem to want to happen? And when you were completely exhausted and disillusioned, the fortunate opportunity presented itself, except now you were tired, overwhelmed and had no energy or enthusiasm left. Having such information ahead of time would offer you the chance to save your energy during quiet, less active time, so that when your luck is more likely, you can seize the opportunity and make the most of it. Since writing my first books on Mudras a while ago, my work has expanded into many different areas, however I always included Mudras into my new ventures. When I designed International Wellness and Spa centers, I included Mudra programs to share these beneficial techniques with a wide audience. I included Mudras into my weekly TV show and guided large audiences thru practice on live shows.

Mudras will forever fascinate me and I have been humbled and excited how many practitioners from around the world have written me, grateful to have these techniques and most importantly really experiencing positive effects in time of need. Therefore it has been a natural idea for me to combine these two of my favorite topics and create a series of Mudra sets for all twelve Astrological signs.

The Mudras depicted in this book are specifically selected for the astrological sign of Aries with intention to help you maximize your gifts and soften the challenges that your celestial map contains.

It is important to know that each astrological chart - celestial map-contains information that can be used beneficially and there are no "bad signs" or "better sings". Your chart is unique as are you. By gaining information, knowledge and understanding what the placements of the planets offer you, your path to self knowledge is strengthened.

I hope this book will attract astrology readers as well as meditation and yoga practitioners and help you utilize the beneficial combination of both these fascinating techniques. Knowledge will help you experience the very best possible version of your life. The biggest mystery in your life is You. Discover who you are and enjoy the journey.

And remember, no matter what life presents you with, don't forget to smile and keep a happy heart. With each experience gained you are spiritually wealthier for it. And that my friend, stays with you forever.

The wisdom gained is eternally imprinted in your soul.

Blessings,

Sabrina

MUDRAS

Mudras are movements involving only fingers, hands and arms. Mudras originated in ancient Egypt where they were practiced by high priests and priestesses in sacred rituals. Mudras can be found in every culture of the world. We all use Mudras in our everyday life when gesturing while communicating and when holding our hands in various intuitive positions. Mudras used in yoga practice offer great benefits and have a tremendously positive overall effect on our overall state of well-being. By connecting specific fingertips and your palms in various Mudra positions, you are directly affecting complex energy currents of your subtle energy body. As numerous energy currents run thru your brain centers, Mudras help stimulate specific areas for an overall state of emotional, physical and mental well being.

INSTRUCTIONS FOR MUDRA PRACTICE

YOUR BODY POSTURE
During the Mudra practice sit in an upright position with a straight spine, with both your feet on the ground or in a cross legged position. Comfort is essential so that you may practice undisturbed and focus on proper practice positions.

YOUR EYES
Keep your eyes closed and gently lightly lift the gaze above the horizon.

WHERE
For achieving best results of ideal Mudra practice it is essential that you find a peaceful place, without distractions. Once your Mudra practice is established, you can practice Mudras anywhere.

WHEN

You may practice Mudras at any time. Best times for practice are first thing in the morning and at bedtime. Avoid practicing Mudras on a full stomach, and after a big meal wait for an hour before practice.

HOW LONG

Each Mudra should be practiced for at least 3 minutes at a time. Ideal practice is 3 Mudras for 3 minutes each with a follow up short 3 minutes of complete stillness, peace and meditation or reflection.

HOW OFTEN

You may practice Mudras every day. Explore various Mudras by selecting a Mudra that fits your specific needs for any given day.

BREATH CONTROL

Proper breathing is essential for optimal Mudra practice. There are two main breathing techniques that can be used with your practice.

LONG DEEP SLOW BREATH

Slowly and deeply inhale thru your nose while relaxing and expanding the area or your solar plexus and lower stomach. Exhale thru the nose slowly while gently contracting the stomach area and pulling your stomach in. Pace your breathing slowly and notice the immediate calming effects. This breathing technique is appropriate for relaxation, inducing calmness and peace.

BREATH OF FIRE

Inhale and exhale thru the nose at a much faster pace while practicing the same concept of expanding navel area and contracting with each exhalation. Unless otherwise noted Mudras are generally practiced with the long slow breath. The breath of fire has an energizing, recharging effect on body and is to be used only when so noted.

CHAKRAS

Along our spine, starting at the base and continuing up towards the top of your head, lie subtle energy centers-vortexes-called charkas, that have a powerful effect on the overall state of your health and well being.
The practice of Mudras profoundly affects the proper function of these energy centers and magnifies their power.

Our subtle energy body is highly sensitive to outside sensory stimuli of sound, aromas, visuals and outside electric currents that constantly surround us. Frequencies that permeate specific locations may attract or bother you. Perhaps you may feel eager to stay somewhere where the energy suits you and yet feel suffocated when the environment does not agree with you. We are all sensitive to energies, but some of us feel them more than others.

A positive blend of energies with another person can create a magnet-like effect, whereas another person's negative unharmonious subtle energy field subconsciously pushes you away.

By leading healthy lives and optimizing the proper function of charkas, you empower your subtle energy bodies adding strength to your physical body, mind and spirit. Destructive behavior like addictions and abuse weakens your Auric field and "leaks" your vital energy. By maintaining a healthy Aura-energy field, you can fine-tune your natural capacity for "sensing" places, situations and people that compliment your energy frequency.
In a state of "clean energy" you achieve capacity for high awareness and become your own best guide.

CHAKRAS IN THE BODY

Base Chakra: Foundation
Second Chakra: Sexuality
Third Chakra: Ego
Fourth Chakra: Love
Fifth Chakra: Truth
Sixth Chakra: Intuition
Seventh Chakra: Divine Wisdom

FIRST CHAKRA
LOCATION: Base of the spine
GLAND: Gonad
COLOR: Red
REPRESENTS:
Foundation, shelter, survival,
courage, inner security, vitality

SECOND CHAKRA
LOCATION: Sex organs
GLAND: Adrenal
COLOR: Orange
REPRESENTS:
Creative expression, sexuality,
procreation, family

THIRD CHAKRA
LOCATION: Solar plexus
GLAND: Pancreas
COLOR: Yellow
REPRESENTS:
Ego, intellect, emotions of fear and anger

FOURTH CHAKRA
LOCATION: Heart
GLAND: Thymus
COLOR: Green
REPRESENTS:
All matters of the heart, love,
self–love, compassion and faith

FIFTH CHAKRA
LOCATION: Throat
GLAND: Thyroid
COLOR: Blue
REPRESENTS:
Communication, truth,
higher knowledge, your voice

SIXTH CHAKRA
LOCATION: Third Eye
GLAND: Pineal
COLOR: Indigo
REPRESENTS:
Intuition, inner vision, the Third eye

SEVENTH CHAKRA
LOCATION: Top of the head - Crown
GLAND: Pituitary
COLOR: White and Violet
REPRESENTS:
The universal God consciousness,
the heavens, unity

NADIS

Your subtle energy body contains an amazing network of electric currents called Nadis. There are 72.000 energy currents that run throughout your body from toes to the top of your head as well as your fingertips. These channels of light must be clear and vibrant with life force for your optimal health and empowerment. With regular Mudra practice you can open, clear, reactivate and re-energize your energy currents.

Your Hands and Fingers

While practicing Mudras you are magnifying the effects of the Solar system on your physical, mental and spiritual body. Each finger is influenced by the following planets:

THE THUMB - MARS

THE INDEX FINGER - JUPITER

THE MIDDLE FINGER - SATURN

THE RING FINGER – THE SUN

THE LITTLE FINGER - MERCURY

MANTRA

Combining the Mudra practice with appropriate Mantras magnifies the beneficial effects of these ancient self-healing techniques.

The hard palate in your mouth has 58 energy meridian points that connect to and affect your entire body.

By singing, speaking or whispering Mantras, you touch these energy points in a specific order that is beneficial and has a harmonious and healing effect on your physical, mental and spiritual state.

The ancient science of Mantras helps you reactivate nadis, magnifies and empowers your energy field, improves your concentration and stills your mind.

ABOUT ASTROLOGY

The word Horoscope   originates from a Latin word
ORA–hour and SCOPOS–view. One could presume that
Horoscope means "a look into your hour of birth". The
precise moment of your birth determines your celestial
set-up.

An accurate astrological chart can reveal most detailed
aspects of your life, your character, your gifts, your future
possible events, challenges that await you, lucky events
that are bestowed upon you, and your outlook for happy
relationships, successful careers, accomplishments, health
and many possible variations of life events. I say possible,
because your decisions will determine the outcome.

There are 12 signs in the Zodiac and your birth-day
reflects the position of your Sun sign. The specific
positions of other planets in your chart are calculated
considering the precise moment-hour and minute and of
course location of your birth. The birth time will reveal
your Rising or Ascending sign, which will further
determine other essential facts of your chart.

The constant transitional movements of the Planets
affect each one of us differently, a time that may be
difficult for some may prove supremely lucky for another
and yet we are interconnected by mutual effects of
continuous planetary movements. Nothing is standing
still, the changes are ongoing. On a different note, a few
slow moving planets connect us in other ways, as they
keep certain generations under specific aspects and
influences. We are all inseparable and in continuous
motion.

There are numerous fascinating ways to use astrology and there is no doubt that the constant motion of all these powerful and majestic Planets in our Solar system affect each and every one of us differently. Astrology can be used as an additional tool to help you continue progressing on the mysterious life journey of self discovery and self-realization.

Remember, the power of decision is yours as is the responsibility for consequences. Make peace with your doubts, pursue your dreams and relish in results.

When the outcome is less than what you expected, learn to pick yourself up and continue on, wiser with knowledge you gained, that alone being a good reason for remaining optimistic. When the outcome surpasses your expectations, well, then you will know what to do…mostly take a breath, smile, and enjoy the moment.

YOUR SUN SIGN

There are 12 signs in the Zodiac. The day of your birth determines your Sun-sign. Most often this is the extent of average person's knowledge and interest in astrology. However, the other aspects in the astrological chart are equally as important and need to be taken into consideration. In this book your main guide is your Sun sign's dispositions, tendencies, weaknesses and gifts. Certainly there are endless combinations of charts and your Sun sign alone will not reveal the complete picture of your celestial map.

For more detailed information and reflection about your chart, you need to know your ascending-rising sign.

Your Ascending-Rising Sign

Your rising sign, also known as the ascendant, reflects the degree of ecliptic rising over the eastern horizon at the precise moment of your birth. It reveals the foundation of your personality. That means that even if you have the same birthday with someone else, your time of birth would create completely different aspects and influences in your chart. No two people are alike. You are one of a kind and so is everyone else. However, you may have some strong similarities and timing aspects that will be often alike. Your rising sign also reveals the basis of your chart and House placements. Your rising sign determines and is in your first house. There are 12 Houses and each depicts precise in-depth information about all aspects of your physical life, emotional make and character tendencies. It is incredibly complex and fascinating. Regarding your Mudra practice in combination with your Astrological Sign, it would be beneficial to know also your Rising sign and apply Mudras that empower your Rising sign as well. For example; if your Sun sign is SAGITTARIUS, but your rising sign is Libra-it would be most beneficial to practice Mudra sets for both signs.

How to use this book

In each book of the *Mudras for the Astrological Signs* series, you will find Mudras for different astrological signs that will help you in most important areas of your life: Health, Love, Success, and Overcoming your challenging qualities. We all have them, as we also all have gifts. This book is specific for the sign of Aries. You may change your Mudra practice daily as needed, and keep in mind, that certain habits or tendencies need a longer time to adjust, change, and improve. Be patient, kind, and loving towards yourself.

MUDRAS FOR TRANSCENDING CHALLENGES

Each one of us has a few character tendencies or weaknesses that are connected to our astrological chart. To help you transcend, overcome and redirect these challenges into your beneficial assets, you can use the Mudras in this chapter.

MUDRAS FOR HEALTH AND BEAUTY

Each astrological sign rules certain areas of your body. The Mudras in this chapter will help you strengthen your physical weaknesses while maintaining a healthy body, and a beautiful, vibrant appearance.

MUDRAS FOR LOVE

The Mudras in this chapter will help you understand your love temperament, your expectations, your longings and how to attract the optimal love partner into your life. It is most beneficial to know how others perceive you in the matters of the heart. It will also help you understand your partner and their astrologically influenced love map.

MUDRAS FOR SUCCESS

The Mudras in this chapter will offer you tools to present yourself to the world in your optimal light. Often one is confused in which direction to turn or where their strength lies. Mudras will help you focus and remember your essential creative desires, help you gain self-confidence and inner security to recognize your desired and destined path. If you know what you want, and your purpose is harmonious for the better good of all, your success is within reach.

MUDRAS
for TRANSCENDING
CHALLENGES

MUDRA of
Good SPEECH

You have the gift of understanding the mysterious and knowing the unknown. Often you find yourself in situations where you guide and teach others about life and old wisdom. It is therefore very important to avoid the unnecessary argument that may discredit the respect you enjoy. Using good tact and finding the best words when speaking and teaching others is essential. This Mudra will help you select and use words with eloquence for a powerful effect.

CHAKRA: Throat- 5

COLOR: Blue

Sit with a straight back. Place your hands in front of your chest, palms apart and all fingertips touching. All fingers are spread apart. Inhale and press together the thumbs and the index fingers. Exhale and relax. Now inhale and press together the thumbs and the middle fingers. Exhale and relax. Continue the same way with the ring and little fingers. Practice for three minutes and finish up the cycle.

BREATH: Long, deep and slow.

MUDRA FOR PATIENCE

You move and think fast and expect the same of others. You can do many things at the same time and again naturally expect the same of others. That may be the reason why you are so impatient with others. Part of being a good teacher is the capacity to teach every single person no matter what level of knowledge they poses or how gifted they are. Teach with care, dedication, precise technique and certainly plenty of patience. Remember how time truly does not exist and you will get to see, do and experience everything you desire, all in due time. This Mudra will help you attain and develop the virtue of patience.

CHAKRA: 6, 7

COLOR: Indigo, white

MANTRA:
EK ONG KAR SAT GURU PRASAAD
(One creator, Illuminated by God's Grace)

Sit with a straight spine. Make circles with the tips of your middle fingers and thumbs. Keep the rest of the fingers straight. Your upper arms are parallel to the floor and elbows are out to the sides. Your hands are at the level of your ears. Fingers are pointing towards the sky and palms are facing front. Hold for three minutes, breathe and keep the elbows nice and high.

BREATH: Long, deep and slow.

MUDRA
FOR PREVENTING EXHAUSTION

When you feel passionate about something there is nothing that can stop you. You work on the project like you are running a marathon and rarely someone can catch up to you or match your perseverance. This is a great quality, but there may be a price with it. You could overextend yourself and then be forced to rest longer than the whole thing would have taken to accomplish, had you chosen a more human pace. Your other tendency to move from one project to next before the first one is completed, gives you a perpetual feeling of being in a hurry and that does not work to your advantage. This Mudra will help you balance your vital energy and prevent possible burnout.

CHAKRA : 3, 4

COLOR: Yellow, Green

MANTRA:

SAT NAM
(Truth is God's Name, One in Spirit)

Sit with a straight back, lift up your arms and grasp your earlobes with the thumb and index fingers. Hold your earlobes tightly and let the full weight of your arms pull on them. Relax and enjoy the immediate effects.

BREATH: Long, deep and slow.

MUDRAS
for HEALTH
and BEAUTY

MUDRA FOR
STRONG NERVES

Your enthusiastic and optimistic nature is something you love sharing with everyone around and near you. You are honest, straightforward and philosophical. That may take some time and effort when conveying to others. Not everyone is eager and ready to take on your jovial and good humored disposition and you will do everything in your power to convince them otherwise. This all takes a tremendous amount of energy which you do have, but let's face it, to be the cheering guide is a demanding proposition especially for your nerves. Learn how to protect, preserve, and nurture your nervous system with proper rest, diet and plenty of peaceful times where you can practice your spiritual meditative techniques. This Mudra is one of those to keep close and a regular part of your maintenance regimen.

CHAKRA : 3, 4

COLOR: Yellow, green

Sit with a straight spine. Lift your left hand at ear level, palm facing out. Connect the thumb and middle finger and stretch out other fingers. Place your right hand in front of the solar plexus, palm facing up. The thumb and little finger are touching while other fingers are straight. **This position is reversed for men**.

BREATH: Long, deep and slow.

MUDRA FOR
RECHARGING

Your body seems indestructible and the never ending supply of energy that you pass onto others is magnetic. However, you are a human and need to be aware of your physical limitations. You are a natural sports enthusiast, remember that you need to adjust your tempo and demands on your body with time.   Do not set over enthusiastic physical goals for yourself. Be tactful when setting limits. Another aspect that requires attention for your optimal health is a very smart diet plan. This will change with time as well, obviously when climbing Mount Everest your diet will differ from at-home holiday time. Recharge your body, mind, and spirit regularly with this Mudra and enjoy long lasting health thru all your adventures.

CHAKRA : 1, 2, 7

COLOR: Red, orange, violet

Sit with a straight spine. Extend your arms in front of you, parallel to the ground, keeping your elbows straight. Make a fist with your right hand and wrap the left hand around your right fist. The bases of the palms are touching and the thumbs are straight up. Hold for three minutes and relax.

BREATH: Long, deep and slow.

MUDRA for
Preventing BURNOUT

Your sign rules the hips and thighs and you are often a gifted sportsman. You are spoiled by this indestructible natural gift especially in your youth and tend to take it for granted. Take the time now to preserve your splendid race-horse condition so that you may enjoy it for many years to come. Perhaps the challenges you set for yourself should be also more intellectual, which is a great stimulant and very important to you as well. This way, you will balance your energy levels and achieve much that you desire.This Mudra will help you harmonize your efforts and prevent burning out your power to quickly. Pace yourself.

CHAKRA : 1, 2 ,3

COLOR: Red, yellow, orange

MANTRA:

OM
(God in His Absolute State)

Sit with a straight back. Bring your forearms up in front of you at heart level and bend your elbows to the side. With the palms facing the ground, fold your thumbs across the palms of each hand till they reach the bases of your ring fingers. Now bend your fingers slightly and touch the backs of your fingertips together, forming a V-shape with your hands. Hold for three minutes and make sure your elbows remain elevated.

BREATH: Long, deep and slow.

MUDRAS
for LOVE

MUDRA FOR OPENING YOUR HEART

Anyone who has ever been in love with you knows what an emotional puzzle you can be. Passionate, wild, and magnetic "soul mate" one moment and "no emotional demands" the next. Words like "always and forever" are banned from your vocabulary. You need your freedom like the air you breathe. However, if and when this phase which may last years, passes, you are ecstatic to settle down. First of all, just relax and let someone near. They won't bite and they won't chain you down. Just enjoy the moment and be. You may like it. This Mudra will help you open your heart and let the loved one in. This is the first step. The rest will follow.

CHAKRA : 4

COLOR: Green

MANTRA:
SAT NAM
(Truth is God's Name, One in Spirit)

Sit with a straight spine and lift your hands in front of your heart with palms and fingers open as if creating a cup. Keep all the fingers stretched and feel healing energy pouring into your fingertips and the area of your heart.

BREATH: Inhale long, deep and slow.

MUDRA FOR
FACING FEAR

As fearless as you are by nature there is one fear you need to conquer. The famous fear of commitment. Yes, you hate being cooped up inside, or committing to a schedule, but falling in love and "losing your freedom" petrifies you to death. It would be wise to relax and remember that you are only a prisoner in your mind where as in love, your power and freedom to conquer the world together is magnified many times over. With the right partner, you will realize that you are always free to fly the sky, but together you have someone special to enjoy the amazing view with. Relax, practice this Mudra and face this imaginary fear. Notice that there is no fear at all, it is just an idea of it. See, now you can breathe together and laugh. What joy!

CHAKRA : 3, 7

COLOR: Yellow, violet

MANTRA:

NIRBHAO NIRVAIR AKAAL MORT
(Fearless, Without Enemy,
Immortal Personified God)

Sit with a straight back. Bend your right elbow and lift the arm up to the level of your face. Face your palm outward, as if taking a vow. Bring your left arm in front of your navel, palm facing up. Concentrate on energy being received into your palms and hold for at least three minutes. Relax and be still.

BREATH: Long, deep and slow.

MUDRA
FOR GUIDANCE

It has finally happened. You've fallen madly in love with your perfect match. What to do? The agony of feeling trapped and the million of other imaginary opportunities you are missing is maddening, but the power of love has taken over. Take some time for yourself and truly connect with your heart. It is love that you wanted and it is love that you got. You are lucky, fortunate and blessed. Now give it your very best effort and enjoy every single second of it. The social butterfly that you are, introduce your lover to your adventurous world and celebrate together.   This Mudra will guide you thru this new experience. Every time you feel overwhelmed, practice this Mudra and receive guidance on how to proceed.

CHAKRA: 7

COLOR: White

Sit with a straight spine. Place your hands together in front of your chest. Little fingers are pressed together to form a cup. Palms are facing towards the sky. Leave a very small opening between the sides of the little fingers. Gently focus your eyes towards the tip of your nose towards the palms. Have a clear question. Hold for three minutes, relax, be calm and wait for a clear answer.

BREATH: Long , deep and slow into your palms.

MUDRAS
for SUCCESS

MUDRA FOR
REJUVENATION

Your magnetic spirit will mesmerize others with your ideas and adventurous nature. You have the capacity to create excitement over a new project and gather a crowd of admirers. All that requires quite a stamina. Make it a regular part of your schedule to properly prepare for demanding events and occasions and "charge up" with Universal energy. After a successfully accomplished mission, take proper rest and relaxation where you can plan your next adventurous escapade and expand your philosophical views. You will need this Mudra to keep up with running in the race you've created.

CHAKRA: 5, 6, 7

COLOR: Blue, indigo, violet

MANTRA:
OM
(God in His Absolute State)

Sit with a straight back. Place both palms of your hands directly on your ears. Circle your hands and massage your ears in a circular motion in the direction away from your face-counter clockwise. Listen to the sound of *"the ocean"* that you are creating with your hands.

BREATH: Long, deep and slow.

MUDRA
FOR PROSPERITY

All that hard work, travel and teaching, but have you managed to deal with the proper pay back? Do not let your wild spirit ignore the realities and business matters. You must descend upon firm ground a few times a year and make sure that all is well and you know who is in charge of your affairs. You. Your wild nature has a bit of a tendency to be irresponsible and careless in financial matters. Your mission to the Moon costs quite a pretty penny, so make sure you don't return to the Earth dirt poor. This Mudra will help you attract, develop and   maintain prosperity on all levels.

CHAKRA : 1, 2, 3,

COLOR: Red, orange, yellow

MANTRA:

HAR HAR
(God, God)

Sit with a straight back. Bring your hands in front of you, fingers together and palms facing down. Press the sides of the index fingers together and hold for a second. Now flip your hands over so that the palms are facing up toward the sky for a second and the edges of the little fingers are touching. Keep repeating and chant the mantra HAR with each change of hand position. Continue the practice for eleven minutes and rest.

BREATH: Short, fast breath of fire from the point of the navel, repeated with each mantra and Mudra movement.

MUDRA FOR
MENTAL BALANCE

While you are ambitious on one hand, yet dislike discipline and schedule on the other, you will enjoy being your own boss and creating some unusual venture of your own. That does take inner discipline on your part and balance of your mind. Create a wise and well thought through business plan that envelops your intellectual and philosophical gifts and expands optimism among others. This Mudra will help you maintain that even mind so that you may pursue your colorful and unusual projects successfully, however you want to, and at your own pace.

CHAKRA : All

COLOR: All

MANTRA:
GOBINDAY, MUKUNDAY,
UDAARAY, APAARAY,
HARYNG,KARYNG,NIRNAMAY, AKAMAY
(Sustainer, Liberator, Enlightener, Infinite,
Destroyer, Creator, Nameless, Desireless)

Sit with a straight spine. Place your hands at solar plexus level in front of you and interlace the fingers backward with palms facing up. Fingers are pointing up and the thumbs are straight.

BREATH: Long, deep and slow.

ABOUT THE AUTHOR

SABRINA MESKO   PH.D.H. is an International and Los Angeles Times bestselling author of the timeless classic *Healing Mudras - Yoga for your Hands* translated into fourteen languages. She authored over twenty books on Mudras, Mudra Therapy, Mudras and Astrology, Holistic Caregiving, Spirituality and Meditation techniques.

Sabrina holds a Bachelors Degree in Sensory Approaches to Healing, a Masters in Holistic Science, a Doctorate in Ancient and Modern Approaches to Healing, and a Ph.D.H in Healtheoloyy from the American Institute of Holistic Theology. She is board certified from the American Alternative medical Association and American Holistic Health Association. She has been featured in media outlets such as The Los Angeles Times, CNBC News, Cosmopolitan, the cover of London Times Lifestyle, The Discovery Channel documentary on Hands, W magazine, First for Women, Health, Web-MD, Daily News, Focus, Yoga Journal, Australian Women's weekly, Blend, Daily Breeze, New Age, the Roseanne Show and various international live television programs. Her articles have been published in world-wide publications. She hosted her own weekly TV show educating about health, well-being and complementary medicine. She is an executive member of the World Yoga Council and has led numerous international Yoga Therapy educational programs. She directed and produced her interactive double DVD titled   *Chakra Mudras* - a Visionary awards finalist.

Sabrina also created award winning international Spa and Wellness Centers and is a motivational keynote conference speaker addressing large audiences all over the world. She is the founder of Arnica Press, a boutique Book Publishing House. Her mission is to discover, mentor, nurture and publish unique authors with a meaningful message, that may otherwise not have an opportunity to be heard. She is the founder of world's only online Mudra Teacher and Mudra Therapy Education, Certification and Mentorship program, with her certified therapists spreading these ancient teachings in over 27 countries around the world.

www.SabrinaMesko.com